THE LOVE LIFE

THE LOVE LIFE
1 Corinthians 13

by
W. Graham Scroggie

KREGEL PUBLICATIONS
Grand Rapids, Mi 49501

The Love Life by W. Graham Scroggie.
Published by Kregel Publications
a division of Kregel, Inc. All rights reserved.

Library of Congress Cataloging in Publication Data

Scroggie, William Graham, 1877-1958.
    The Love Life.

    Reprint of the 1935 ed. published by Pickering & Inglis,
London, which was issued as 24 of the Worldwide library of
sterling Gospel books.
    1. Bible. N.T. 1 Corinthians 13—Criticism, interpretation,
etc. 2. Love (Theology)—Biblical teaching. I. Title. II. Series:
Worldwide library of sterling Gospel books; 24.
BS2675.S37   1980   227'.2'077   79-2551
ISBN 0-8254-3733-4

Printed in the United States of America

Contents

"Belovèd, let us love: love is of God;
In God alone hath love its true abode.

Belovèd, let us love: for they who love,
They only, are His sons, born from above.

Belovèd, let us love: for love is rest,
And he who loveth not abides unblest.

Belovèd, let us love: for love is light,
And he who loveth not dwelleth in night.

Belovèd let us love: for only thus
Shall we behold that God loveth us."

HORATIUS BONAR

Outline

9

III. **THE PERMANENCE AND VICTORY OF LOVE** (verses 8-13).

1. A CLIMAX IS REACHED (verse 8a).

2. A CONTRAST IS PRESENTED (verses 8b-12).
   - (i) An Affirmation (verse 8b).
     - (*a*) The Fact Affirmed.
     - (*b*) The Limits of the Fact.
   - (ii) An Explanation (verses 9, 10).
     - (*a*) The Reason why the "gifts" must pass away (verse 9).
     - (*b*) The Time at which the "gifts" shall pass away (verse 10).
   - (iii) An Illustration (verse 11).
     - (*a*) The Illustration Itself.
     - (*b*) The Thing Illustrated.
   - (iv) A Confirmation (verse 12).
     - (*a*) Our Present and Future Seeing (verse 12a).
     - (*b*) Our Present and Future Knowing (verse 12b).

3. A COMPARISON IS INSTITUTED (verse 13).
   - (i) The Excellence of the Three Virtues.
   - (ii) The Permanence of the Three Virtues.
   - (iii) The Greatest of the Three Virtues.

4. A COURSE IS ENJOINED (chap. xiv., verse 1a).
   - (i) Why? The Reason.
   - (ii) How? The Method.

Introduction

(*a*) THE SETTING OF THIS CHAPTER.

(*b*) THE SIGNIFICATION OF "LOVE."

Introduction

BEFORE considering in detail the contents of this wonderful passage, there are two preliminary matters of importance which claim our attention, namely, the setting of this chapter and the signification of love.

(*a*) THE SETTING OF THIS CHAPTER.

Chapters xii, xiii, and xiv of this Epistle form a distinct division of it, and treat of the subject of Spiritual Gifts; chapter xii tells of the rich endowment of the gifts; chapter xiii tells of their vital energy; and chapter xiv tells of their worthy exercise. Thus between the endowment in chapter xii and the exercise in chapter xiv is placed this sublime Song, revealing that love alone can safeguard the *use* (chapter xiv) of that which is *bestowed* (chapter xii).

It has been pointed out that "on each side of this chapter the tumult of argument and remonstrance still rages. But within the chapter all is calm; the sentences move in almost rhythmical melody; the imagery unfolds itself in almost dramatic propriety; the language arranges itself with almost rhetorical accuracy. We can imagine how the apostle's amanuensis must have paused to look up into his master's face at the sudden change in the style of his dictation, and see his countenance lighted up as it had been the face of an angel, as this vision of divine perfection passed before him. This is the earliest detailed description of this element of goodness, and we cannot help wondering that it was Paul, and not John, who gives it to us. To the minds of both these great apostles, amidst all their other diversities, *Love* represented the chief fact and the chief doctrine of Christianity, and we cannot doubt that both derived it from a common source— the character and example of Christ. "

The Church at Corinth "came behind in no gift," but it was sadly lacking in love, as a reading of this Epistle will show. But the Spirit of God here declares that if one has not love, he has nothing; and that if one has love, whatever else he may lack, he has what matters most.

(*b*) THE SIGNIFICATION OF LOVE.

This naturally leads us to the consideration of the other preliminary point, the Signification of Love. The Revised Version has done well to substitute the word "love" for the word "charity" of the Authorised Version and the Vulgate, because this latter expression has changed its meaning. It usually means one or other of two things: either almsgiving, as in the phrases "an act of charity," "an object of charity," or "a charitable institution"; and love is contrasted with this idea in verse 3. Or it means toleration, as when we speak of "a charitable construction," or "charity with our neighbours." But there may be both almsgiving and toleration without love, so that the word "charity," as we now understand it, is a wholly inadequate rendering of the word in this chapter, and wherever else it occurs in the New Testament.

It will be well for us at once to observe that love is not here defined, but just displayed. "There are times when definition is destruction. Whoever questioned the beauty of the sunset? But who can define it? The astronomer can give us the mathematics of it, and I doubt not there is mathematics in the sunset, but there is no sunset glory in the mathematics. There is a chemistry of colours, but there is no wistful healing light in that chemistry. Beauty defined is beauty destroyed." But though love cannot be defined, it may be described and displayed, and by giving careful attention to these expressions of it we shall come to apprehend and appreciate its true nature.

Let it be said then, first of all, that

(i) *Love is Spiritual.*

There are three words in the Greek language which are translated "love." One of these tells of the love of passion, of lust, of sensual desire. The word occurs in the Old Testament in Esther, Ezekiel, Hosea, and in Proverbs, but never in the New Testament. So base were its associations that Christianity could find no use for it. The second of these words tells of the love of impulse, of affection, of natural inclination. We find it in such words as "philosophy" and "Philadelphia." It occurs in both Testaments, and speaks chiefly of our love for one another, of affection among relations and friends. But the third word, that which occurs in this chapter and so often in the New Testament, is expressive of character determined by will, and not of spontaneous natural emotion. It denotes the love which chooses its object with decision of will, so that it becomes self-denying, or compassionate devotion to and for the same. The word is used in all places where the direction of the will is the point to be considered. Thus "love," and not "affection," is used of the Christian attitude toward enemies. Christianity took up this word and infused into it an entirely new meaning, which distinguishes it from all that is lustful or merely emotional. This word is absolutely unstained by any evil association. So the first thing to apprehend is the spiritual quality of love.

Now let it be said, in the second place, that (ii) *Love is Divine.*

This third word has the unique honour of being the only substantive noting a moral attribute which is predicated simply and without explanation or limitation of God Himself. "God is Love." Therefore, we are not singing to an abstraction when we sing George Matheson's moving hymn:

> "O Love that wilt not let me go,
> I rest my weary soul in Thee!"

or Charles Wesley's:

> "O Love Divine, how sweet Thou art!
> When shall I find my willing heart
> All taken up by Thee?"

or Horatius Bonar's:

> "Eternal Love, in Thee we rest,
> For ever safe, for ever blest,"

but we are worshipping Him Who not only does love, but is Love, whose character is holy Love.

It is this fact, that "God is Love," which gives the word "love," as it is used in the New Testament, its heavenly quality. From these

Writings we learn that this love is discoverable essentially only *in* God, is displayed perfectly only *by* God, and is derived mediately only *from* God.

And because it is spiritual and divine, it must be added, in the third place, that

(iii) *Love is Indestructible.*

The apostle here says that while other things pass away, love lasts, it never fails. It is not dependent upon, nor is it affected by anything outside of itself. It is content to bestow itself upon the worthy and unworthy alike, and in the human heart it moves upward and outward: *upward* to God, and *outward* to men. In the chapter before us it is the latter of these actions which is presented.

Kagawa has gone to the root of the matter when he says that Love is the Law of Life. It is the basal principle of spiritual health; the supreme constructive force of life; the maker of character, the revealer of truth, the secret of development, and the pledge of fulfilment. The distinction between natural and supernatural love, between human affection and the love which is spiritual, divine, and indestructible, is well brought out in the risen Christ's conversation with Peter on the shore of the Galilean lake early one morning. This is the substance of the conversation. Jesus asked

Peter: "Lovest thou Me more than these?"
Peter replied: "Yea, Lord, Thou knowest that
I have an affection for Thee." Jesus a second
time asked: "Lovest thou Me?" and Peter
replied: "Yea, Lord, Thou knowest that I
have an affection for Thee." The third time
Jesus asked: "Hast thou an affection for Me?"
and "Peter was grieved because the third time
Jesus said unto him, Hast thou an affection
for Me?" He was not grieved because Jesus
asked him three times, but because the third
time Jesus came down to his word, as he had
not risen to Christ's word. "And he said unto
Him, Lord, Thou knowest all things; Thou
knowest that I have an affection for Thee."
This remarkable passage shows that Peter's
faith in himself had been so severely shaken
by his denials of his Lord that he dare not now
profess this spiritual and indestructible love
for Him, but he can confess his human affection.
But after Pentecost the apostle rose to the
higher level, and proved his love by his death.

1

The Pre-eminence and Value of Love

1 Corinthians 13:1-3 R.V.

"If I speak with the tongues of men and of angels, but have not love, I am become sounding brass, or a clanging cymbal. And if I have the gift of prophecy, and know all mysteries and all knowledge; and if I have all faith, so as to remove mountains, but have not love, I am nothing. And if I bestow all my goods to feed the poor, and if I give my body to be burned, but have not love, it profiteth me nothing"

ANALYSIS

1. Love should be sovereign in the human heart (verse 1).

   Controlling our emotional powers.

2. Love should be sovereign in the human mind (verse 2).

   Controlling our intellectual powers.

3. Love should be sovereign in the human will (verse 3).

   Controlling our volitional powers.

The Pre-eminence and Value of Love

TURNING to this Hymn of Love, observe that it is in three main parts. Verses 1 to 3 disclose the Pre-eminence of Love; verses 4 to 7 detail its Prerogatives; and verses 8 to 13 declare its Permanence. Part 1 reveals Love's Value; part 2 recounts its Virtue; and part 3 records its Victory. In the first stanza is a vision of life without love; in the second, is a vision of love as the secret and strength of character; and in the third, is a vision of love as the goal of life.

Let us now consider the first of these three parts. In verses 1 to 3 we have a vision of life without love. We are bidden behold a life crowned with powers and services of which a man scarcely dare dream, and yet, for want of love, all is vain and empty. Here the search-light of love is thrown upon man's great powers of emotion, and intellect, and will, and each of these at its best is seen to be valueless without love. These qualities are distinguished in the statement by the recurring phrase "but have not love," in verses 1, 2, and 3.

First of all, then, it is said that

1. LOVE SHOULD BE SOVEREIGN IN THE HUMAN HEART (verse 1).

"If I speak with the tongues of men and of angels, but have not love, I am become sounding brass, or a clanging cymbal." Love should be in possession of our entire emotional nature. "Speaking with tongues" is the expression, according to the context, of rapturous delight, of utterance under the strongest emotion. For a moment, the apostle supposes himself to be in possession of this power in its highest form and fullest measure. He speaks "with the tongues of men *and* of angels;" he employs the language of terrestrial and celestial excellency, he uses the widest and fullest range of expression imaginable, and this as indicative of the highest and intensest emotion. Yet, he says, such a gift, unaccompanied by love, makes its exercise to be worthless, for this gifted but loveless man is only "a noisy gong" or "a clanging cymbal." Though the utterance of this gift included all that both worlds could express of the great and glorious, yet, without love to harmonise them, they would be but jarring and unmeaning discords. The power of expression is not determined by the length of a man's vocabulary, but by the depth of his heart.

Poetry, sentimentality, and fine speaking can be no compensation for the lack of divine love. We might, conceivably, have the mouth of a Demosthenes, or of a Chrysostom, yet, if it were without the Spirit of Christ, we would fail. Of what use is loveless eloquence? The power to talk is not only worthless, but dangerous, if unaccompanied by love. Love is the one language which has universal meaning, and, like nature, it needs no words. Language without love is noise without melody; it is the clang of a gong, and not the music of an organ. Chatter is of no use without charity, nor is sound without soul. Language may arrest the attention, but only love can satisfy the heart. Jesus said: "The first of all the commandments is, Thou shalt love"; and Paul says that that is the sum of them all, and the fulfilment of the law.

In the next place, it is said that

2. Love should be Sovereign in the Human Mind.

"If I have the gift of prophecy, and know all mysteries and all knowledge; and if I have all faith, so as to remove mountains, but have not love, I am nothing." That is, love should be in control of all our intellectual powers. Now, observe carefully the four things here named, things which belong to our intellectual rather than to our emotional, or volitional activity. By "prophecy" is meant the power to interpret and declare. A prophet is one who interprets life to men in the terms of its eternal significance, and so, prophecy comes to mean inspirational power. By "mysteries" we are to understand the apprehension of Divine secrets, the discernment of that which is spiritual. By "knowledge" is meant intelligence in the truth; and by "faith" the quality which gives us mastery over life's difficulties, firmness of belief. Again, the apostle supposes himself to possess each of these gifts in its ideal perfection, to discern all the counsels of God, to possess all insight into truth, and to exercise all faith conceivable, and withal, by inspirational power—by prophecy or preaching—to share his gifts with others. Yet, he says, all this notwithstanding, if I be wanting in love, "I am nothing."

Balaam shows that inspirational power is possible apart from love. Caiaphas shows that spiritual discernment is possible apart from love. Judas shows that much knowledge of divine things is possible apart from love; and

James and John show that a certain kind of
faith is possible apart from love. It is love
alone that makes these gifts of any real value
to the possessor. These things are not to be
despised, but without love they are ultimately
worthless. Love alone is the proof of spiritual
life, and the touchstone of Christian character.
The things here detailed are gifts, but love
is *a grace*, and we know that one may possess
gifts without grace, or may possess grace
without gifts. What we should learn from the
passage before us is that it is better to have
this grace without gifts, than to have all the
gifts without this grace. The absence of love
implies selfishness; and inspirational power,
insight, knowledge, and faith may be very
selfish. Faith without love has done much to
embitter the life of the world. Wherever in the
same life you find deep convictions and shallow
sympathies, you have the possibility of much
unconscious cruelty. Loveless faith may remove mountains from its own path, only to
set them down in its brother's path. Selfishness can be intelligent, respectable, and even
spiritual. The world has had its loveless pro-
phets, loveless scholars, loveless pioneers,
people who have had power without grace;
but it is not these who are fondly remembered
and finally crowned.

It has been solemnly said, "In our day, too, one may be a celebrated theologian, the instrument of powerful revivals, the author of beautiful works in the Kingdom of God, a missionary with a name filling the world; yet, if in all these things the man (or woman) is self-seeking, and if it is not the divine breath of love which animates him (or her) in God's eyes, this is only *seeming*, and not *being*." What such a man does may be of value to the Church, but he profits not thereby where love is wanting. The apostle says that such a man is "nothing," that is, his character has no real worth.

And, finally, in this paragraph which treats of the Pre-eminence and Value of love, we are taught that

3. LOVE SHOULD BE SOVEREIGN IN THE HUMAN WILL (verse 3).

The whole passage is psychologically sound and true. "If I bestow all my goods to feed the poor, and if I give my body to be burned, but have not love, it profiteth me nothing." Love should dominate the faculty of the will. In verse 1 the thought is related to our emotional power; in verse 2, to our intellectual power; and in verse 3, to our volitional power; and these are our principal faculties. In the kingdom of the soul these should co-operate with one another, but they can do so effectively only as love is in control of them all. Only love can harmonise and direct our many powers, and only as love does so, can life fulfil its true end.

Now two things are here named, than which nothing more extreme in the exercise of the will is conceivable. These are the distribution of all that one possesses, and the surrender of oneself to flames of fire, the absolute sacrifice of property and of life. The apostle conceives of himself as making this sacrifice only to say, that if these actions were not motived and directed by love, they brought no profit to himself. It may seem incredible that sacrifices such as these would or could be made by a loveless person, and yet, that is what the passage supposes, and not without some ground. Dean Stanley has said: "Who that ever witnessed the almsgiving in a Catholic monastery, or in the Court of a Spanish or Sicilian Bishop's or Archbishop's palace, where immense revenues are syringed away in farthings to hordes of beggars, but must feel the force of the apostle's half satirical, 'If I bestow all my goods?'"

And with regard to the second idea, this is known to have been done. There is the story of one, Sapricius, a Christian of Antioch, who, on his way to martyrdom, refused to forgive his enemy Nicephorus. And it is on record that an Indian, a Buddhist in the time of Augustus, burnt himself. His tomb at Athens may have been seen by the Apostle Paul, with this inscription: "Zarmochegas, the Indian from Bargosa, according to the ancient customs of India, made himself immortal, and lies here."

The point of the passage is that conceivably a Christian might make the supreme sacrifice from some motive other than love. Actions in themselves have no intrinsic value. Their worth, both as manifestations of character, and as spiritual gain to the actor, depend entirely upon their motive, and while the sense of duty may be a worthy one, the highest and noblest motive is love. The pages of Christian history show that men will fight and die for Christianity, who will not live in its spirit, which is love. The Lord's indictment of the Ephesian Church is a warning to us all: "I know thy works, and thy toil and patience, and that thou canst not bear evil men . . . and thou hast patience, and didst bear for My Name's sake, and hast not grown weary. But I have this against thee, that thou didst leave thy first love."

What, then, is life without love? The

apostle's fivefold "if" and fourfold "all"
create such a person as never lived, one who has
matchless eloquence, profound insight, wide
knowledge, tremendous faith, the will to utmost
sacrifice, yet, he says, though all of these
qualities were found in a single person, if he
were without love, what he did would profit
him nothing, and he himself would be nothing.
In the sight of God all gifts without love are
worthless, but love, even where there are no
gifts, is everything. We must, of course, be
careful to bear in mind that the reference is
not to natural amiability, or the spirit of
benevolence, but to the love which is spiritual,
divine, and indestructible. This is the greatest
of all great things, having which, one has all,
and lacking which, he has nothing.

Let us well contemplate the possibility of
love controlling all our heart, and mind, and
will; dominating all our feelings, and thoughts,
and choices. Then let us yield to this sublime
control, and so experience the will of God for
us, that we shall love with all our heart, and
mind, and strength.

2

The Prerogatives and Virtues of Love

1 Corinthians 13:4-7 R.V.

"Love suffereth long, and is kind; love envieth not; love vaunteth not itself, is not puffed up, doth not behave itself unseemly, seeketh not its own, is not provoked, taketh not account of evil; rejoiceth not in unrighteousness, but rejoiceth with the truth; beareth all things, believeth all things, hopeth all things, endureth all things"

ANALYSIS

1. Love is not Hasty, but Patient.
2. Love is not Inconsiderate, but Benevolent.
3. Love is not Envious, but Content.
4. Love is not Boastful, but Unostentatious.
5. Love is not Arrogant, but Humble.
6. Love is not Rude, but Courteous.
7. Love is not Selfish, but Self-forgetful.
8. Love is not Irritable, but Good-tempered.
9. Love is not Vindictive, but Generous.
10. Love is not Malevolent, but High-principled.
11. Love is not Rebellious, but Brave.
12. Love is not Suspicious, but Confident.
13. Love is not Despondent, but Undiscourageable.
14. Love is not Conquerable, but Indomitable.

The Prerogatives and Virtue of Love

THE second part of this Hymn of Love treats of its Prerogatives and Virtue. But before examining these verses (4-7), we should see their relation to what has just been said.

In vv. 1-7, two pictures are drawn, showing, in vv. 1-3, what the Church at Corinth *was*, and should not have been; and in vv. 4-7, what the Church at Corinth *was not*, and should have been.

In vv. 1-3 is a description of Gifts without Love, and in vv. 4-7 a description of Love without Gifts.

"That in vv. 4-7, nothing is said about spiritual gifts, and that yet the passage retains its full force, even though gifts be absent, proves that, whereas gifts without love are worthless, love, even without gifts, retains its value undiminished."

In vv. 1-3, attention is called to a number of great qualities: eloquence, inspiration, insight, knowledge, faith, service, and sacrifice, and to these as being all possessed in full measure by one man, who, it is declared, if he lack love, nothing gains, and nothing is.

These seven excellencies are like seven ciphers, which, without a digit before them are nothing in the total; but which, with the digit "love" in front, would represent ten million in moral value. It is love which gives to all other qualities their moral value, and without it they are inconsiderable; but it, even without them, is inestimable.

This picture of love is not the dream of an artist, but the work of a photographer; and Christ is the original. He was and is incarnate Love, Whom we may so address without becoming abstract or impersonal in thought. To love like this is to be like Christ, and the degree of our failure is the measure of our unlikeness to Him.

Almost all the instructions of the New Testament are suggested by some occasion, and are adapted to it. We have in this chapter, for instance, not a methodical dissertation on Christian love, but an exhibition of this grace as contrasted with extraordinary gifts which the Corinthians inordinately valued. Those traits of love are, therefore, adduced which stood opposed to the temper which the Corinthians exhibited in the use of their gifts. They were impatient, discontented, envious, inflated, selfish, indecorous, suspicious, resentful, censorious, and these things are all and always contrary to love.

And now let us address ourselves to this wonderful passage, which, as we see, treats of the Prerogatives and Virtue of Love (vv. 4-7).

Here we are shown what are the ingredients of love, or, to use Henry Drummond's figure, we are shown the colours which together make the bright warm light of love.

"Love suffereth long, and is kind; love envieth not; love vaunteth not itself, is not puffed up, doth not behave itself unseemly, seeketh not its own, is not provoked, taketh not account of evil, rejoiceth not in unrighteousness, but rejoiceth with the truth; beareth all things, believeth all things, hopeth all things, endureth all things."

In these words the virtue of love is first summarised, and then scrutinised; it is seen first to be negative and passive, and then positive and active.

The former is love in an attitude of *restraint*, and the latter is love in an attitude of *constraint*. First of all it is represented as *holding back*, and then as *letting go*. Both these qualities are attributed to God in Romans ii. 4, where we read of His "longsuffering" and "goodness."

Here, then, the first two statements about love may be regarded as summarising what immediately afterwards is detailed, and altogether there are fourteen lines of description, a double seven. Let us look at each of these in its negative and positive aspects.

1. *Love is not Hasty, but Patient.*

It "suffereth long." The word denotes the long waiting-time during which the man refuses to give way to anger. "Longsuffering" is a passive quality. It implies victory over a just resentment. Love is "longsuffering" when, having been wronged, it is patiently silent. Love is "longsuffering" when, in the face of injuries and wrongs, it persists and endures and waits.

2. *Love is not Inconsiderate, but Benevolent.*

It "is kind." If "longsuffering" is a passive quality, this is an active quality. If "longsuffering" is the victory over a just resentment, this is the victory over idle selfishness and comfortable self-pleasing.

These negative and positive sides of love enable one to "leave his rights and wrongs with God, and find the leisure of unselfishness wherein to serve his brethren."

To endure only may be but a triumph of obstinacy, but to endure and be kind is a triumph of grace.

The love of God is not only infinitely patient, but also infinitely beneficent.

Love must be kind.   You can no more have love without kindness than you can have springtime without flowers.   The greatest thing a man can do for his Heavenly Father is to be kind to some of His other children.

3. *Love is not Envious, but Content.*

It "envieth not."   That is, it is not idly vexatious at the superiority of others, begrudging them their endowments and privileges and advantages.

We recognise that life is full of inequalities, and only love can be trusted to contemplate them and remain content.   Where there is not love, almost certainly there will be envy. Envy was the cause of the first murder in human history, and it is the last vice to be eradicated out of the human heart.   Bacon has called it "the vilest affection and the most depraved."

But love does not envy, because it is content, and it is content because its heart is set not on earthly gifts and gains; and because it finds its joy, not in getting, but in giving.

Great illustrations of unenvying love are seen in the attitude of Jonathan towards David, and of John the Baptist towards Jesus.

Only one thing truly need the Christian envy,

and that is the large, rich, generous soul which "envieth not."

4. *Love is not Boastful, but Unostentatious.*

It "vaunteth not itself." This means, as Dr. Moffatt translates it, that love "makes no parade"; it does not "show off" any supposed superiority of its own.

Ostentation is the display of gifts really possessed, and must be distinguished from the boast of gifts not possessed. Ostentation desires to gain the applause of others, and to win their admiration; but this, love never does.

We speak of "empty boasting." There is no other kind of boasting. The very nature and essence of a boast is emptiness. Boasting is always an advertisement of poverty.

We have only to think of the things of which the world boasts, to know that no man has anything to boast of. There is no brag, no swank, no swagger about love. It is too big for that. It was the frog in Æsop's fable that tried to blow itself up into the size of a cow. Boasting is a vulgarity, and love is never vulgar.

5. *Love is not Arrogant, but Humble.* It "is not puffed up." Love knows nothing of presumptuous self-satisfaction, of pride with contempt of others (and these two things always go together), of inflated vanity. It "gives itself

no airs"; is never haughty, but humble and gracious. The greatest men have always been humble.

When Dr. Cairns was Head of the Theological College in Edinburgh, he was offered the Principalship of the University there, but declined it, preferring to serve his Church in a humbler way. On public occasions, he was accustomed to stand back and let others pass him, saying, "You first, I follow."

When he was dying he said farewell to those whom he loved, but his lips continued still to move. They bent to catch the final word, which doubtless was spoken to Him Who was dearer to him than life—"You first, I follow.

Such lowliness is one of the richest ingredients of love, and in its presence pride becomes an impertinence and an offence.

6. *Love is not Rude, but Courteous.*

It "doth not behave itself unseemly." Love is not disorderly, or eccentric, or indecorous it is never lacking in propriety or politeness. Do let us learn that there is such a thing as the etiquette of the Christian life, and only love knows and practises it.

Love is the eternal fitness of things. It ever seeks the best in the best way. Love is perfect good in perfect touch with life. For each of us, each hour, there is but one best way, the way of love.

Courtesy is just love in little things. Why should we so often do good badly? Why should we practise one virtue at the expense of another? Why should our honesty flout our charity? Why should our candour outstrip our sympathy? Why should our earnestness threaten our patience? Out of all such happenings there comes into our life the unseemly thing.

There is so much awkward piety, so much blundering goodness, so much unattractive sanctity, so much unlovely religion. But why? For lack of love!

The Psalmist, describing the blessed man, says: "He bringeth forth his fruit in his season; his leaf also shall not wither," and surely the Christian's foliage is just this quality of courtesy and seemliness!

7. *Love is not Selfish, but Self-forgetful.*

It "seeketh not its own." He who loves does not grasp at his own rights, nor see the utility of all things only in his own pleasure and advancement, disregardful of the good and pleasure of others. Love "seeketh not its own," but finds its joy and wealth in self-forgetfulness for the sake of service.

The good of others is always in love's motive,

whatever it may be doing. "Its learning is for the light of others; its toil is for the good of others; its prayer and faith and sacrifice are for the cleansing and the comforting of others." Love realises itself in self-lessness. "It seeketh not its own."

8. *Love is not Irritable, but Good-tempered.*

It "is not easily provoked." Now, bad temper is not a mere infirmity of nature, nor merely a matter of temperament, though it is often thought so to be. Of bad temper Drummond has said, "no form of vice, nor worldliness, nor greed of gold, nor drunkenness itself, does more to unchristianize society than evil temper. For embittering life, for breaking up communities, for destroying the most sacred relationships, for devastating homes, for withering up men and women, for taking the bloom off childhood; in short for sheer gratuitous misery-producing power, this influence stands alone."

It is generally the self-centred people who are touchy and easily exasperated.

Love can and, given occasion, should be angry, but there is a difference between righteous anger and irritability. Christ was at times angry, but never irritable.

This vice is often the one blot on an otherwise noble character. Too often it is the vice of the virtuous.

9. *Love is not Vindictive, but Generous.*

It "thinketh no evil." By this is meant that, whereas love keeps a diary of all the good it receives, it does not keep a record of the wrongs done to it. These things it does not lay up in its memory with the intention of getting square with them some day.

It is tragic to find David on his dying-bed recalling the wrongs that Joab had done him, and hearing again the curses of Shimei showered upon him as he fled from Jerusalem. He had all these things written down in his account books; but love does not keep such records. Love is generous in her forgetfulness.

It is said of Abraham Lincoln that he never forgot a kindness, but that he had no room in his mind for the memory of a wrong.

There is a morality of memory, and love keeps a list of its creditors, but none of its debtors.

10. *Love is not Malevolent, but High-principled.*

It "rejoiceth not in unrighteousness, but rejoiceth with the truth." Dr. Moffatt translates this, "Love is never glad when others go wrong: love is gladdened by goodness."

Love never makes capital out of other's faults, and does not delight in exposing the weakness of others. Nevertheless, love is opposed to sin, and grieves and weeps over it.

It is the ally of the truth, and in sheltering the sinner it will never fail to condemn his sin.

What a man rejoices in is a fair test of his character.   To be glad when evil prevails, or to rejoice in the misfortunes of others, is indicative of great moral degradation.   Alas, there is such a thing as "malignant joy," and it is reflected in a remark of La Rochefoucald, that "there is something not altogether disagreeable to us in the misfortunes of our best friends." That is an acute remark which we may well contemplate.   But love knows nothing of this. Here she meets truth, and they share their joy together.

11. *Love is not Rebellious, but Brave.*

It "beareth all things."   "Beareth" here has been thought to have the force of "covereth," *i.e.*, veiling, as far as may be, the seamy side of life.   But that idea is in the previous quality, "Love is never glad when others go wrong," and, therefore, does not talk about it.   "Beareth" is therefore the better translation, and this quality has both an active and passive meaning.

Passively, love "bears" by suffering wrong done to itself without retaliating.   We remember it is written of Christ that, "when He was reviled, He reviled not again."   And *actively*, love "bears" when it gets under the load of life, and bravely carries it.

Probably the passive aspect dominates in our passage.

"Love is strong in its silences"; it patiently endures what it has to suffer. It is not shaken by any sort of ingratitude, but is proof against all reproaches and hardships. The word used here is highly pictorial; it is employed of holding fast, like a watertight vessel; it is used of a roof which does not leak; it is used of troops defending a fortress, and it is used of ice bearing weight, and not giving way.

This does not mean that love acquiesces in all that it bears; but it does mean that it bravely stands up to life, and chooses to suffer rather than to rebel.

12. *Love is not Suspicious, but Confident.*

It "believeth all things." This does not mean that love is blind and credulous, that it is easily deceived; but it does mean that it is not suspicious; that it is entirely alien to the spirit of the cynic, the pessimist, the anonymous slanderer, the secret detractor.

Love takes the best and kindest view of all men, in all circumstances, as long as it is possible so to do. Love endeavours to estimate the force of varying circumstances; it studies motives, and makes all possible allowances.

This is what Phinehas and the Israelites *did not* in the matter of the altar which the two and a half Tribes built on the border of the Land.   This is what Thomas Carlyle *did* when he pleaded so eloquently for a tempered judgment of Robert Burns.   He says, "Granted the ship comes into harbour with shrouds and tackle damaged; the pilot is blameworthy; he has not been all wise and all powerful; but to know how blameworthy, tell us first whether his voyage has been round the Globe, or only to Ramsgate and the Isle of Dogs."

It is this quality in love which helps men and women to become what they should be. There is a tendency in all life to adjust itself to the judgment passed upon it.

There are some people who seem incapable of believing in disinterested goodness: who view every action, however good, with suspicion. On the other hand, it was because Christ saw in outcasts hidden splendours, infinite capabilities lying buried, that He became the Friend of publicans and sinners, and this belief in them was a factor in their salvation.

"Through the tired ranks of the vanquished, through the throngs of the disheartened, across the trampled fields of life strewn with wasted efforts and battered dreams, love passes, still believing in all things, and in the light of that brave faith, many a man stretches out his hand for his sword, and finds it worth gripping, even though it be a broken one. "

13. *Love is not Despondent, but Undiscourageable.*

"It hopeth all things. " We have seen love "bearing" because it "believes. " But when it is disappointed in the object in whom it believes it yet hopes for better things of him in the future, even when others have ceased to do so. Large views and large hopes go together.

Love *hopes* even when it cannot find firm ground for *faith*. To hope when faith has been disappointed is a greater thing than ever to have believed.

Back of love's hopefulness, and justifying it, is the fact that on the one hand God is seeking man, and on the other hand that man is made for God, and so love never despairs of anybody.

It has rightly been said that love does not "hope all things" by juggling with the evidence of its senses. It does not try to persuade itself that the thief is honest, or the libertine chaste, or the worldling heavenly-minded. But it grapples to its soul the fact that every man was *made* for honesty, and purity, and the heavenly vision; and "where it cannot find room for its faith amid the narrow and sad realities of the hour, love slips its hand into the hand of hope and carries its faith onward into the ampler air of good and holy possibility."

Just because these Christian virtues are vitally related, love is impossible apart from faith and hope, and so, it *"believeth* all things" and *"hopeth* all things."

14. *Love is not Conquerable, but Indomitable.*

It "endureth all things." Love "bearing" all things refers to its attitude when it does not receive *what is due* to it; but love "enduring" all things refers to its attitude when it receives *what is not due* to it, that is, ill-treatment. This quality is the crown of all that has gone before.

Now look at these four things:

Love *bears,* silently suffers, and actively hopes, and it does so because it *believes,* putting the best construction upon the conduct of others, and expecting much of every one. When this faith is betrayed love still *hopes,* looking to man's need and God's grace; and when such hope is sadly disappointed, love continues to *endure;* this is the very climax of love's courage and optimism.

Love holds its ground in the day of defeat. At midnight it keeps its face to the dawn. When others faint and give way, love holds on.

The best of all other efforts grows weary in

its labours to get God's will done on earth as it is done in heaven, but love persists in spite of all delays. This is its final triumph.

We must all acknowledge then, that love is the greatest of all great things in the world; not hasty, but patient; not inconsiderate, but benevolent; not envious, but content; not boastful, but unostentatious; not arrogant, but humble; not rude, but courteous; not selfish, but self-forgetful; not irritable, but good-tempered; not vindictive, but generous; not malevolent, but high-principled; not rebellious, but brave; not suspicious, but confident; not despondent, but undiscourageable; not conquerable, but indomitable.

I have said that this portrait of love is not the work of an artist, but of a photographer; it is a portrait of Christ. He is the great example of longsuffering, infinitely patient because eternal. His habit of life is summarised in the testimony that "He went about doing good." He never desired to possess any good for Himself alone; neither did He ever begrudge others any good which they possessed. He envied not. The greatness of Christ consisted quite as much in what he suppressed as in what He exhibited, as in the veiling of His glory, and in His restraint in working miracles. There was no "showing off." He displayed no vanity, conceit, pride, or contempt of others. There was perfect seemliness in all He did; a perfect fitness of things. Though the most approachable of men, there was never any lack of dignity or self-possession. He did the right thing always, in the right way, and at the right time.

He was the very negation of selfishness. He lived for others. He was never exasperated at wrong done to Himself; and there was much. He was never vindictive. He never retaliated. He had the Divine power of forgetfulness of wrongs done to Himself. He yearned over the erring and sinful, and shielded them from those who would make capital of their sin. He patiently bore the wrong done to Him by honour and love withheld; and at the same time He put His shoulder under the load which others were carrying, and helped them to carry it. He never misjudged, because He judged not by the outward appearance. He saw faith wherever it existed, and believed wherever belief was possible. He never abandoned any soul, but hoped for, and won the prodigal, the harlot, and the thief. He calmly endured all opposition and persecution, and prayed on the Cross for His enemies.

Now the business of our lives is to have these things fitted into our character. That is the supreme work to which we need to address ourselves in this world, to learn to love.

But how can we learn so great a lesson? Only by practice. Looking at pictures does not make a man an artist; and listening to music does not make one a musician; the paints must be mixed, and the instruments must be played. In like manner we can love in no other way than by loving.

Says Matthew Henry: "How lovely a thing would Christianity appear to the world if those who profess it were more actuated and animated by this divine principle, and paid a due regard to a command on which its blessed Author laid a chief stress."

"A new commandment give I unto you, that ye love one another, as I have loved you. By this shall all men know that ye are My disciples." Let us therefore love as never before!

3

The Permanence and Victory of Love

1 Corinthians 13:8-12 R.V.

"Love never faileth: but whether there be prophecies, they shall be done away; whether there be tongues they shall cease. Whether there be knowledge it shall be done away. For we know in part, and we prophesy in part; but when that which is perfect is come, that which is in part shall be done away. When I was a child, I spake as a child, I felt as a child, I thought as a child; now that I am become a man, I have put away childish things. For now we see in a mirror darkly; but then face to face: now I know in part; but then shall I know, even as also I have been known"

ANALYSIS

1. A CLIMAX IS REACHED (verse 8a).

2. A CONTRAST IS PRESENTED (verses 8b-12).

   (i) An Affirmation (verse 8b).
   - (*a*) The Fact Affirmed.
   - (*b*) The Limits of the Fact.

   (ii) An Explanation (verses 9, 10).
   - (*a*) The Reason why the "gifts" must pass away (verse 9).
   - (*b*) The Time at which the "gifts" shall pass away (verse 10).

   (iii) An Illustration (verse 11).
   - (*a*) The Illustration Itself.
   - (*b*) The Thing Illustrated.

   (iv) A Confirmation (verse 12).
   - (*a*) Our Present and Future Seeing (verse 12a).
   - (*b*) Our Present and Future Knowing (verse 12b).

The Permanence and Victory of Love

Love and Gifts Contrasted

LET us recall again the content of this great Song. In verses 1-3, it is shown that without love all other gifts are worthless; in verses 4-7, the various qualities of love are displayed; and in verses 8-13, love is declared to be supreme over all the gifts. In the first part, the theme is *the Pre-eminence of Love*, showing its Value; in the second part it is *the Prerogatives of Love*, showing its Virtue; and in the third part it is *the Permanence of Love*, showing its Victory.

The heart of this sublime Song is verse 8a, "Love never faileth." The context before leads up to this; and the context after flows out from it.

The Climax Reached in this declaration (verse 8a), and the Course Enjoined in chap. xiv. 1a, are set forth in *seven words*, the number of completeness, and these seven begin and end with the words, "The love."

"The love never fails . . . pursue the love."
Between the Climax Reached in verse 8a,
and the Course Enjoined in xiv. 1a, a Contrast
is Presented in vv. 8b-12, and a Comparison
is Instituted in verse 13. We are now to
consider the Climax and the Contrast, that
is verses 8-12.

1. A Climax is Reached (8a)

"Love never faileth." The greatest thing
that can be said about love is that *it lasts.*
"Never," is a long word, but love reaches to
its uttermost meaning: "it stands for, and
gathers into its heart, all life's everlasting
treasure and meaning." Love never fails.
This word has several shades of meaning, all
illuminating in this connection.

It means that love never falls to the ground,
as do the petals of a faded flower, because there
are in love no elements of decay; it means that
love never loses its strength, as does a weary
traveller who gives up a journey; it means that
love never leaves its place, as do falling stars;
and it means that love never drops out of
line, as exhausted soldiers on the march fall
by the way. All love's comrades may fail
and fall, but she doggedly and patiently
marches on.

This love has its origin in heaven, and its

perfect incarnation in Christ. "Having loved His own which were in the world, He loved them *unto the end.*" An endless end.

Such is Christ's love that nothing can cut off His people from it, "neither death, nor life, nor angels, nor principalities, nor powers, nor things present, nor things to come, nor height, nor depth, nor any other created thing can separate us from the love of God which is in Christ Jesus our Lord."

Throughout all time and eternity we shall be apprehending more fully what are the breadth, the length, the depth, and the height of the love of Christ, which passeth knowledge.

The love of passion quickly fails; it is like the flame of burning straw, one fierce blaze, and then all is over: but true love lasts; it is like the steady glow of the eternal sun.

The "love of God," which He "sheds abroad in our hearts," knows no decline or decay; it never becomes a fond memory.

Mrs. Browning, in her poem entitled, "Loved Once," asks which of all earth's sounds is the most lamentable; the sigh of misfortune, or the sharp notes of strife, or the sob of the mourner, or the "fall of kisses on unanswering clay"? and she concludes that more lamentable than any of these is the pathetic cry, "I loved once."

"And who saith, 'I loved once'?
Not angels, whose clear eyes love, love foresee,
Love, through eternity,
And by 'To Love' do apprehend 'To Be.'

"Not God, called Love, His noble crown-name casting
A light too broad for blasting:
The Great God, changing not from everlasting,
Saith never, 'I loved once.'

"Oh, never is 'Loved once'
Thy Word, Thou Victim Christ, misprizèd Friend!
The Cross and curse may rend,
But having loved, Thou lovest to the end.

"This is man's saying—man's: too weak to move
One spherèd star above,
Man desecrates the eternal God-word Love
By his 'No more,' and 'Once'."

Love never fails, and

"They never loved who dreamed that they loved once."

"Love looks beyond the bounds of time and space;
Love takes eternity in its embrace."

Love is deathless. Disappointments, dis-illusionments, defeats, cannot rob it of its strength: in the face of all these it continues to *bear*, to *believe*, to *hope*, and to *endure*. "Love never fails."

2. A Contrast is Presented (8b-12)

In these four verses there is, firstly, an Affirmation (verse 8b), that prophecies, tongues and knowledge shall change or pass away,

but that love shall abide. This is followed by
an Explanation (verses 9, 10), that the partial
must give place to the perfect, and the transitory to the eternal. This is followed by an
Illustration (verse 11) that life here, and life
hereafter, stand related to one another as do
childhood to manhood. And this again is
followed by a Confirmation (verse 12) that
necessarily all things here and now are imperfect, but there and then, in God's im-
mediate presence, they will be absorbed into
eternal fulness. A pregnant passage indeed.

These four points now claim our attention.

(i) AN AFFIRMATION (verse 8b).

Look first at the Fact Affirmed, and then
at the Limits of the Fact.

(a) *The Fact Affirmed.*

"But whether there be prophecies, they
shall be done away, whether there be tongues,
they shall cease; whether there be knowledge,
it shall be done away." Three "gifts" are
referred to, of those named in verses 1-3,
Prophecy, and Tongues, and Knowledge.

By interpretation, these are among the
special "gifts" bestowed by the risen Lord upon
His Church in the Apostolic Age. "Tongues"
is the language of ecstasy; "prophecy" is the
power to interpret and communicate spiritual
truth; and "knowledge" is special under-

standing of the Divine mysteries. But by application it may be said that "tongues" stands for all languages; "prophecy" tells of illumination and inspiration for preaching; and "knowledge" speaks of all thought-progress. Now, mark what is affirmed of these. Prophecy and knowledge, Paul says, are to be "done away," and tongues are to "cease."

It is important to mark the change of word, because it shows that "done away," spoken of prophecy and knowledge, does not mean cessation.

"Tongues," that miraculous gift, is altogether to disappear, and it is not referred to again, in what follows, as are prophecy and knowledge (verse 9).

The reason for the ceasing of tongues is in their ecstatic character. "The only ground for ecstatic transport is that we are not yet living fully in the reality of the Divine. When we live fully in God, we are in Him without going out of ourselves."

This is why there was no ecstasy in the life of the Lord. He lived fully in God.

The gift of tongues is for ever to cease, and the context makes it clear that the time referred to is the future life. Prophecy and knowledge, however, are not "to cease," but are to be "done away." And now let us be careful to observe

(b) *The Limits of the Fact.*

What, it may be asked, are we to understand by the word translated, *"done away"*? It means that these "gifts" are to be superseded, that they are to give place to something higher and larger. Prophecy as the "gift" of insight, possessed now only by the few, will then be possessed by all, and in perfection: and for the reason that prophecy as preaching will no longer be needed, for all shall dwell in God's unveiled presence. In like manner, the "gift" of knowledge shall be superseded, that is, it shall be replaced by a knowledge that shall be common and comprehensive. We are taught more about Heaven and our state and estate there in this passage than in any other single passage in the New Testament.

The difference between knowledge here, and hereafter, will be as the difference between the hearing of an object and seeing it. The imperfect will melt into the perfect. That this is what is meant becomes quite clear from the use of the same word "done away" in verse 12. — "when I became a man I *did away* with the things of the infant."

Relative then, to the subject before us, tongues shall for ever cease, prophecy and

knowledge shall be perfected, but love shall
for ever abide the same. Prophecy and knowledge are for ever changing in measure and
form, and all these measures and forms shall
ultimately give way to something that shall
be final: but love, from the beginning and
eternally is unchanging, and ultimately will
absorb all the "gifts" into a stronger, more
united and effective life. Love is greater than
all the "gifts," not because it *eclipses* them,
but because it *includes* them.

These gifts are not disparaged; they are good
things in themselves; but in their present form
they do not last. But love is imperishable,
it is never outgrown, it never becomes obsolete,
it is the only permanent wealth of life. All
other things shall slip from our hands, but the
love we practise and cherish we shall keep
eternally.

In the next four verses, 9-12, the apostle
leaves the subject of love, to show *why* and
when the "gifts" must be superseded. There
follows, therefore

(ii) AN EXPLANATION (verses 9, 10).

"For we know in part, and we prophesy in
part; but when that which is perfect is come,
that which is in part shall be done away."

What we have anticipated is now plainly
declared, namely,

(a) *The Reason Why the Gifts must Pass Away.*

It is because the *partial* and *imperfect* cannot be *permanent*. Understanding and knowledge are progressive. This is true of knowledge generally. There is no such thing as a stock of knowledge, fixed, defined, and complete. Knowledge is ever growing, and expanding and developing.

What one generation calls knowledge the next generation calls ignorance. There are editions of the "Encyclopedia Britannica" which can be bought for a few shillings, just because they are out-of-date.

The advance which has been made during the last fifty years in philosophic and scientific knowledge has made for our generation a new world; and advances will be made to-morrow which will antiquate to-day. We should be very modest when we speak of *our knowledge*. And what is true of knowledge in general, is true also of spiritual knowledge. "We know only in part, and we prophesy only in part."

This was true of the saints in pre-Christian times: "God by divers portions, and in divers manners, spake" to them; and they learned of His redeeming purpose "bit by bit." And although, now, in Christ, a flood of light has been released, yet all around are confines of darkness; so that we know only "in part." Even revealed knowledge is marked by imperfection, which, however, is not in the things revealed, but in the range and mode of the revelation. We *"know in part"* of necessity, not of choice; but if we *love in part*, it is of choice, and not of necessity.

Knowledge is like the changing form and substance of the body from infancy to manhood; but love is like the principle of life which persists throughout.

Our knowledge at every stage is fragmentary, partial, preparatory, and therefore it must give way to that which is to come; but love is perfect from the beginning.

And now our attention is called to

(b) *The Time at which the Gifts shall Pass Away* (verse 10).

"When that which is perfect is come." Quite obviously the "perfect" never comes in *this world*, and, therefore, the reference must be to the heavenly estate; so that partial and imperfect prophecy and knowledge are coextensive with the Christian dispensation. Not until Christ's advent can that which is perfect come. Then the partial things of time shall be displaced by the perfect things of eternity. When the top form of the school is reached, the text-books of the lower forms are put aside.

The torches we use in the night are of no use when the morning comes. Some flowers have a sheath during the early period of their growth, but when the flower is perfected the sheath drops away.

When things have served their purpose, they pass away, but because the purpose of love is eternal, it never passes away.

"Aye, and when prophecy her tale hath finished,
  Knowledge hath withered from the trembling tongue,
 Love shall survive, and love be undiminished,
  Love be imperishable, love be young."

But let us bear in mind that the partial prepares for, and moves towards the perfect; that it serves a real purpose, an indispensable purpose. The twilight of morning prepares for midday. The winter heralds the spring, and the spring the summer. The perfect could not come, but for the partial. Back of manhood is youth, back of youth is childhood, and back of childhood is infancy.

Let us not despise the stages which lead to the goal. Partial and imperfect good will not pass away in extermination, but in absorption into some higher thing, as the pools left on the beach at ebb-tide are swallowed up in the fulness of the ocean when the tide comes sweeping back again in flood.

Meanwhile we may love with the love which

is pure, lofty, patient, generous, undiscourageable, and imperishable. Upon everything
else are the marks of imperfection and trans-
ciency, but on love is the hall-mark of eternity.
"Love never fails." It is the greatest of all
great things. Therefore, to love is to live.

And now follows:

(iii) AN ILLUSTRATION (verse 11).

"When I was a child, I spake as a child, I
felt as a child, I thought as a child; now that I
am become a man, I have put away childish
things." The apostle resorts to a natural and
personal illustration to show that the law of
spiritual growth is the same as the law of
natural growth, that is, growth by the process
of development and transformation.

Look first at the illustration, and then at
that which it illustrates.

(a) *The Illustration Itself.*

"When I was a child, I spake, felt, thought
as a child; now that I am become a man, I
have put away childish things." How great is
the difference between childhood and manhood
in respect of speech and feeling and thought!
Compare the impression made on the mind of
a child, and on that of an astronomer, respec-
tively, by the contemplation of the starry sky!
The impression made on the mind of a child
is not scientific, but for a child it is a just and

true one. The child's view is neither irrational, nor false, it is simply inadequate. Every child is an "Alice in Wonderland," and lives in a world of phantasy and imagination: and how sad a world it would be if it were otherwise! It was the tragedy of Coleridge's life that he never was a child. But childhood is only a stage in life, and not its goal. A person who is a man in years while still a child in mind and habit is just a monstrosity. How sweet to hear the simple chatter of a child, but how sad to hear an adult chattering like a child! The law of growth is transformation by development. The faculties of the child acquire a higher mode of activity, so that the previous mode is rendered useless. The man has taken up into his maturity all the essential elements of his childhood: nevertheless, he has "put away" his former childish mode of speaking, and feeling, and thinking.

That is the Illustration. Now consider

(b) *The Thing Illustrated.*

As with natural, so is it with spiritual childhood and maturity. It is most important to see the precise point of the comparison. Spiritual maturity is not, as natural maturity, regarded within the limits of time. It is a wholly wrong conception of the thought to regard childhood here as meaning the early years of our Christian life, and maturity the later years; or to regard childhood as pointing to the early centuries of the Church, and maturity as pointing to the later centuries. The point of comparison is safeguarded in verse 10 in the words "that which is in part"—that is childhood, and "that which is perfect"— that is maturity; and in verse 12, in the words "for now"—that is the time of childhood on earth; "but then"—that is the time of maturity in heaven. From this we see that spiritual *childhood* is co-extensive with this life, and that *maturity* is attained only in the next life.

All the spiritual gifts belong to the state of spiritual childhood, but when Christ comes, and maturity is reached, they will no longer be needed, and so will be "put away." The truth here taught is, therefore, threefold: namely, first, as childhood is the basis of manhood, so spiritual being here is the foundation of spiritual being hereafter: second as childhood is in order to manhood, so partial attainments here are with a view to perfect attainment hereafter; and third, as childhood is absorbed in manhood, so inadequate apprehension here will give place to full understanding hereafter.

Just as the things of manhood are so far beyond the things of childhood as to altogether supersede them, so shall the Christian's maturity in heaven supersede and transcend his childhood on earth. The future will be a development and expansion of the present. As the oak is the product of the acorn, and as the river is the fulness of the fountain, so the man is the product and fulness of the child. The future shall as immensely transcend the present as midday transcends the dawn, and as the end of revelation transcends its beginning.

What the apostle is affirming and illustrating is then that, whereas prophecy and knowledge must necessarily be superseded, love remains ever the same, it never changes, and it never fails. It alone can bring us to life's true stature, and to the fulness of its powers.

By the grace of love we are to outgrow the puerilities and follies of human nature; we are to come into vital touch with all the currents that flow through human life; we are to attain—not here, but hereafter—to the vigorous endurance of spiritual maturity, and to the large and catholic knowledge and sympathy of "the life which is life indeed." Therefore, "beloved, let us love one another, for love is of God, and every one that loveth is born of God, and knoweth God. He that loveth not, knoweth not God, for God is love."

And now follows,

(iv) A CONFIRMATION (verse 12),
of what has been affirmed. Recall again the line of the thought. The subject of verses 8-13 is the Permanence of Love. The passage begins with "Love never fails" (8a), and ends with "Love abides" (13), and between these assertions it is shown that the "gifts" will either pass away, or assume higher forms. This is first affirmed (verse 8b), then explained (verses 9, 10), then illustrated (verse 11), and then confirmed (verse 12).

The subject in this verse (12) is still the child and the man, the partial and the perfect, the present, and future, and the apostle confirms what he has just said by contrasting our present and future seeing and knowing.

(a) *Our Present and Future Seeing* (12a).

"Now we see through a mirror in an enigma; but then, face to face." The contrast is between seeing indistinctly and seeing clearly. Seeing indistinctly in the present, and clearly in the future. Ancient mirrors were usually of polished metal, and only reflected dimly and imperfectly; and, further, that which was seen in the mirror, by an illusion seemed to be behind it, hence the expression *"we see through a glass."* The expression "in an enigma" which is the Greek, and "darkly" (R.V.), means *obscurely*, and the reference is to our acquaintance with things *mediately*, and not *immediately*.

It is an interesting point whether the "mirror" is *subjective* or *objective* in significance, that is, whether it points to dullness of apprehension in us, or to dullness of reflection in the revelation, or to both. Certainly our apprehension of revealed truth is dull; but is not the medium of that revelation also dull? The clearest revelation of the things of God in words, is as an enigma when compared to sight. Everything is comparative. The revelations made to Moses were clear in comparison to the communications made to others by visions and dreams. But the Writings of Moses were enigmas compared to the Revelation contained in the Gospel; and the Gospel itself is obscure compared to the lucid medium through which we shall see hereafter.

The present unveiling of God is relatively obscure. Take *Creation*: Creation cannot perfectly reflect God; we cannot explain its many mysteries, its destructive cyclones, its deadly diseases, its volcanic eruptions, its ruinous earthquakes. And *History* cannot perfectly reflect God. It is full of problems which we cannot solve; ghastly wars, successes of the wicked, and sufferings of the innocent. And even *Scripture* cannot perfectly reflect God,

because of the relative obscurity in the manifestations of divine things; and the faultiness
of our apprehension of the truth. In comparison
with that which we *shall see*, here and now
Nature dimly reflects God's *glories*; *History*
dimly reflects His *government*; and *Scripture*
dimly reflects His *grace*.

Now we see but glimpses, and hear but
whispers of the great truths upon which our
higher life and deathless hopes depend.

We do not see Divine things themselves,
but only in symbols and words, which but
imperfectly express them.

Human language dealing with Divine facts
can only represent them indirectly, metaphori-
cally, enigmatically, under human images,
and as illustrated by visible phenomena.

But one day, says the apostle, we shall see
"face to face." There will no longer be dullness
of apprehension, nor of reflection, but all will
be clear. The vision itself will be direct; the
organ of vision will be unimpaired; the atmos-
phere will not be clouded by sin; and the
conditions of life there will secure uninter-
rupted communion.

And to emphasise this, the apostle contrasts
(*b*) *Our Present and Future Knowing* (12b).

"Now we know in part; but then shall we
know fully, even as we are fully known."

This is not a repetition of the previous statement, but extends the thought.

In this estate our knowledge is limited in range, because our powers are limited, our opportunities are restricted, and our life is circumscribed. Further, we do not know all that is revealed, and what we do know is imperfectly apprehended.

> "I know the night is heavy with her stars—
> 　So much I know—
> I know the sun will lead the night away,
> 　And lay his golden bars
> Over the fields and mountains, and great seas;
> I know that he will usher in the day
> 　With litanies,
> Of birds and young dawn-winds. So much I now—
> 　So little though."

But when that "which is perfect is come," we shall know perfectly things which here we have but begun to understand. No doubt, entire new fields of knowledge will be opened to our eager minds. But chiefly, God will be revealed for our contemplation and understanding in a manner and measure impossible to us here.

Knowledge now is fragmentary, successive, analytic, discursive, but then it will be intuitive, central, distinct, complete. Now we know progressively and by effort, but then we

shall fully know, and shall completely understand the meaning of our salvation.

This statement, elaborate and profound,
is intended to set forth more clearly the sub-
limity and vast superiority of love over everything else. All the features of the present
economy shall pass away, but "Love never
faileth."

Let us therefore prepare here and now for
what awaits us there and then.

I will conclude with a few lines of Miss
Amy Carmichael's, which recently were given
to me, and which, I trust, we shall make
our prayer:

> "Love of God, Eternal Love,
>   Shed Thy love through me.
>   Nothing less than Calvary's love
>   Would I ask of Thee.
>   Fill me, flood me, overflow me,
>   Love of God, Eternal Love,
>   Shed Thy love through me."

4

The Permanence and Victory of Love

THE THREE VIRTUES COMPARED

1 Corinthians 13:13-14:1a

"But now abideth Faith, Hope, Love, these three; but the greatest of these is Love. Follow after Love"

ANALYSIS

3. A Comparison is Instituted (verse 13).

    (i) The Excellence of the Three Virtues.

    (ii) The Permanence of the Three Virtues.

    (iii) The Greatest of the Three Virtues.

4. A Course is Enjoined (verse 14, 1a).

    (i) Why? The Reason.

    (ii) How? The Method.

The Permanence and Victory of Love

The Three Virtues Compared

L ET us recall just for a moment again, how the apostle is treating this great theme.

In verses 1-3, he speaks of the Pre-eminence and Value of Love; in verses 4-7, of the Prerogatives and Virtue of Love; and in verses 8-13, of the Permanence and Victory of Love.

We are now to conclude our consideration of the last of these, Love's Permanence and Victory. Here observe again that a Climax is Reached in verse 8; a Contrast is Presented in verses 8-12; a Comparison is Instituted in verse 13; and a Course is Enjoined in Chap. xiv. 1a.

Let us look at verse 13, in which

3. A Comparison is Instituted (13)

"Now abideth faith, hope, love, these three, but the greatest of these is love." The apostle ends his Song on the top note. He has kept his most splendid chord for the last. Three things Paul says pass away—prophecy, and tongues, and knowledge; and three things remain—faith, and hope, and love. In the previous paragraph the supreme greatness of love has been shown by way of contrast (verses 8-12), but here it is shown by way of comparison, not with the "gifts," but with love's companion virtues—faith and hope.

Let us, therefore, consider these three things —the excellence, the permanence, and the greatest of the three virtues—faith, hope, and love.

(i) THE EXCELLENCE OF THE THREE VIRTUES.

Faith, Hope, Love. Recall the association of these in the Writings of Paul. In Romans v, 1-5: "Being justified by *faith* . . . we rejoice in *hope* . . . because the *love* of God is shed abroad in our hearts." In Col. i. 4, 5: "We heard of your *faith* in Christ Jesus, and of the *love* which ye have to all the saints, for the *hope* which is laid up for you in heaven." In 1 Thess. i. 3: "Remembering without ceasing your work of *faith*, and labour of *love*, and patience of *hope*," and in chap. v. 8: "Putting on the breastplate of *faith* and *love*, and for an helmet, the *hope* of salvation." Love is not magnified by our minimising the greatness of faith and hope.

Consider for a moment,

(a) *The Greatness of Faith.*

Faith is trust, upon evidence, which leads to action, and is both human and divine. *Human faith* is an universal possession which enters into all our relations with our fellows. It is the quality upon which the whole fabric of our social, commercial, and governmental structure rests. Without it, civilised life would be impossible. *Divine faith* is absolute dependence on, and happy confidence in God, and is the possession of Christians only. Indeed, only by faith can one become a child of God. "As many as received Him, to them gave He the right to come children of God, even to them that *believe* on His Name." Religion itself is dependent on faith, for "He that cometh to God must *believe* that He is, and that He is a rewarder of them that diligently seek Him." The *fact* of faith is illustrated in the Old Testament; and the *doctrine* of faith is expounded in the New Testament.

And think of,

(b) *The Greatness of Hope.*

Hope is a gladly and firmly-held prospect of future good, and it also is human and divine.

How tremendous a quality is *Human hope*! Imagine this world of beings without expectation, without outlook, without hope! Notwithstanding that all earthly hope is accompanied with uncertainty, and experiences disappointment, yet, we continue to hope, and did hope fail us the lamp of life would go out.

But far greater a quality is *Divine hope*! Human hope, at its best, is confined to this world and its things, but divine hope reaches far beyond the present order of things, and sees horizons brighter than the sun. Without such hope Christianity would be impossible, for "in hope were we saved," and "if we hope for that which we see not, then do we with patience wait for it." Christian hope is not a dark, perhaps, but a sunlit certainty; it is not a vague guess, but a glad assurance.

And what can be said of,

(c) *The Greatness of Love*?

That is the subject of the whole chapter, in which it is shown that all the "gifts" without love are nothing; that love even without the "gifts" is sufficient, and that whereas the "gifts" are transient, love abides. The least that can be said of love is, that it is one of the first three greatest things in the world. How great then are these three, and how vitally related!

Faith is pre-eminently Paul's theme, Hope is pre-eminently Peter's theme, and Love is pre-eminently John's theme. Faith possesses the past, Hope claims the future, and Love rules the present. Faith sees Christ having come, Hope sees Christ yet to come, and Love sees Christ ever abiding. Faith realises, Hope visualises, and Love vitalises.

Though separated in the representation, faith, hope, and love are really inseparable companions, closely united, not only to every Christian, but also to each other. "What, indeed, is faith without hope and love? A cold conviction of the intellect, but without life-awakening power in the heart, or mature fruit in the life. Without hope, faith would never behold heaven; but even if it could enter therein, heaven would lack its highest bliss.

And what is hope without faith and love? At most an idle dream, from which we soon shall sadly wake; a fragrant blossom in the garden, fading before it has brought forth fruit. And, lastly, what is love without hope or faith? The welling forth, perhaps, of natural feeling, but in no degree a spiritual principle of life. If love believes not, it must die; and if it hopes not in the same measure as it loves, it is then the source of unparalleled suffering. Thus, whichever of these three sisters we would separate from the others, in so doing we have subscribed her death-warrant; nay, even if two of them remain together, the brightness of their beauty is dimmed when the third has disappeared. "

> "So Faith shall build the boundary wall,
>   And Hope shall plant the secret bower,
>   That both may show magnifical
>   With gem and flower.

> "While over all a dome must spread,
>   And Love shall be that dome above;
>   And deep foundations must be laid,
>   And these are Love."

Let us think, in the second place, of

(ii) THE PERMANENCE OF THE THREE VIRTUES.

"Now abideth. "   Here is,

(a) *A Declaration.*

"Now abideth faith, hope, love. " All three abide.   A whole school of commentators, beginning with Chrysostom, has interpreted the word "now" in this passage as of *time*, as in verse 12, but unquestionably it is used, not in a temporal, but in a logical sense; it is the equivalent of "so then. " It is not contrasted with the "then" of verse 12, but indicates a summing up of the subject. The Corinthians had thought the "gifts" were the abiding things; but Paul shows them that these must pass away; and then he says: "In conclusion, in reality, this is what abides, and by no means what you suppose. "

It is curious that this meaning has been so generally missed by readers of the passage. Learned readers, as well as unlearned, have failed to observe it. You may frequently see it assumed in hymns (and hymnology is not always theology) and other religious literature that faith and hope, instead of being associated with love in this quality of permanence, as Paul declares them to be, are contrasted with it, in that they are transitory while love is eternal.

"Faith will vanish into sight,
Hope be emptied in delight,
Love in Heaven will shine more bright."

Such language is plausible enough to be generally accepted. But it is at variance with Paul's view. The passage we are considering is not one of doubtful meaning; no competent interpreter could question that Paul's purpose is to say that faith, hope, and love all abide; and that by "abide" he means that they have not the changing and transitory character which belongs to the other things of which he has been speaking. It is true that he is asserting the supreme glory of love; it is greater, he says, than faith and hope, but these two sister graces share with it the significant distinction that they all abide.

The chief point, then, to be noticed in this statement, is the permanence it ascribes to those graces of which it speaks. It represents "faith and hope and love, these three," as all alike abiding.

Therefore "now" in our passage does not mean "now in time," for then "these three" would in no wise differ from the "gifts."

And now "abideth." This word must receive its full force. It equals the "never faileth" of verse 8a, and is contrasted with the "shall be done away" of verse 8b.

Whatever, therefore, is said of love is said also of faith and hope. When Paul takes three words, and couples them with a verb in the singular, he is not making a slip of the pen, or committing a grammatical blunder which a child could correct. But there is a great truth in that piece of apparent grammatical irregularity; for the faith, the hope, and the love, for which he can afford only a singular verb, are thereby declared to be in their depth and essence one thing, and it, the triple star, abides, and continues to shine; the three primitive colours are united in the white beam of light. Do not correct the grammar, and spoil the sense, but discern what he means when he says: "Now *abides* faith, hope, love." For this is what he means, that the two latter come out of the former, and that without it they are naught, and that it without them is dead,

Faith and hope and love are one in essence, these are a trinity in unity, and therefore they are co-extensive with one another.

But is it so that faith and hope abide? Shall not faith give place to sight? And shall not hope give place to fruition? Scripture nowhere says they shall. Indeed, it is certain that they will *not*, if the continuity of life be a truth.

So after this Declaration is,

(*b*) *An Implication.*

Just because faith and hope, equally with love, are vital conditions of our relationship to God, they must abide while the relationship lasts. Faith and hope are not mere adjuncts of human life, but are fundamental terms of our personal existence, and therefore must abide as long as God and the soul abide. Just because eternally we shall remain finite, depending upon the infinite, faith and hope as well as love, on which our spiritual life is conditioned, must abide.

And in this Declaration and Implication is,

(*c*) *A Revelation.*

A revelation of at least two things. The first of these is that,

(*i*) The Future Life shall be Progressive.

As by faith and hope we acquire what is divine, and as there never can come a time when there shall be no further need to acquire, we shall never be able to dispense with faith and hope. Faith shall go on for ever to possess God more fully; and hope shall never cease to catch new perspectives of glory.

We must be careful not to confuse the *eternal* and the *final*—eternity does not mean finality—to reach finality would be to fall short of eternity. We must also be careful to distinguish between *perfection* and *finality*. In heaven there will be perfection, but there will be differences of attainment, even as "one star differeth from another star in glory." Each has all the blessedness he can contain, but capacities will vary, and in each case there will be progress from stage to stage.

"In My Father's House are many *mansions*," that is, "resting places," a figure which refers to those "stations" on the great roads, where travellers could get rest and refreshment, before proceeding on their journey. The notions both of *repose* and *progress* are in the word, but these, in heaven as on earth, are conditioned upon faith and hope.

Let it be said again that it is no more a Scriptural idea that hope is lost in fruition than it is that faith is lost in sight. Rather, the future presents itself to us as the continual communication of an inexhaustible God to our progressively capacious and capable spirits. In that continual communication there is continual progress. Wherever there is progress there must be hope. And thus the fair form which has so often danced before us elusive, and has led us into bogs and miry places and then faded away, will move before us through all the long avenues of an endless progress, and will ever and anon come back to tell us of the unseen glories that lie beyond the next turn, and to woo us further into the depths of heaven and into the fulness of God. Hope "abides." Every fresh acquisition of God will make fuller acquisition possible; every new height of glory scaled will reveal yet more glorious heights beyond; and the eternal means of our progress there, as here, will be faith and hope and love. These alone are the things of the present which shall for ever remain, because they are the essential elements of Christian character.

This brings to light another truth, namely, that,

(*ii*) Only Christian Character Abides.

The "gifts" are not of the essence of character, but faith, and hope, and love are. As nothing else is said to "abide," we must believe that these three are, in some sense, a complete description of our abiding state.

In this verse Paul has found an absolutely complete and satisfactory formula for the Christian character. Faith, hope, and love, with love in the place of honour—is not this Christianity in a nutshell. What the cardinal virtues, Justice, Fortitude, Prudence, and Temperance were to pagan antiquity; what Liberty, Equality, and Fraternity were to the French Revolutionists; what the Rights of Man were to the founders of the American Republic; what the three stages in the spiritual ascent, Purification, Illumination, and Union with God, have been to mystics of all ages and countries—that Faith, Hope, and Love have been and are to all Christians. The imitation of Christ means the life of faith, the life of hope, the life of love. Faith and hope and love will last after all other things have dropped away. At the gates of death we shall lay down for ever the various weapons with which God has armed us to fight for Him—the gifts, and all other capacities for usefulness—but we shall carry through those gates the moral and spiritual character which the conflict of life has developed within us, and the three constituent elements which enter into Christian character are faith and hope and love.

When the last day is ended,
    And the nights are through,
When the last sun is buried
    In its grave of blue;

When the stars are snuffed like candles,
    And the seas no longer fret;
When the winds unlearn their cunning,
    And the storms forget;

When the last lip is palsied
    And the last prayer said—
Love shall reign immortal
    While the worlds lie dead!

But Love an everlasting crown receiveth;
For she is Hope, and Fortitude, and Faith,
Who all things hopeth, beareth, and believeth.

We turn now to the last of the great truths given to us in this passage:

(iii) The Greatest of the Three Virtues.

"The greatest of these is *love*." We have in this chapter standards of value. Some gifts are greater than others. Faith and hope and love are greater than the gifts. Love is greater than faith and hope. Paul does not say that of these three love is the most *durable*; it is not, for all three abide—but love is *the greatest*. Not only greater than the passing things, but also the greatest of the permanent things; not only the greatest thing on earth, but also the greatest thing in heaven; not only the greatest thing in time, but also the greatest thing in eternity.

But naturally we ask in what respects is love greater than faith and hope? In three respects at any rate. First, because whereas faith and hope are means to an end,

(a) *Love is an End in Itself.*

Faith and hope are means of attainment, but love is that which is attained. Faith and hope belong to the race, but love is the prize. We cannot rest in faith and hope without their being diminished, because, were that possible, our eyes would be on the means instead of on the end; but we can and should rest in love, for in this God Himself rests (Zeph. iii. 17). For this reason love is supreme.

But there is another reason, namely, because, unlike faith and hope,

(b) *Love is Sacrificial.*

We do not and cannot exercise faith and hope effectually for others, but only for ourselves. No doubt by faith and hope we exercise an influence beyond ourselves individually, but they are chiefly for ourselves. Our faith and hope in God bring *us* spiritual gain, but love is for others. We ourselves need it, but we get it, and keep it, only as we give it. We cannot bestow upon others our faith or our hope, but we can bestow upon others our love. For this reason also, love is supreme.

But there is yet another reason, namely, because,

(c) *Love is of the Divine Essence.*

Faith and hope are not. You cannot describe God in terms of faith and hope. God the all-knowing does not *believe*; and God the all-possessing does not *hope*; but you can describe God in terms of *love*. "God *is* love." Faith and hope are things to *have*, but love is something to *be*. Faith brings life; hope presses on to fulness of life; but love *is* life. To love is to compass life's last meaning, and to reach its last arbitrament. Love is the keyword of all religion. There is nothing in all the Christian creed that cannot be interpreted by means of it, and in terms of it. There is nothing that has any clear meaning or real worth apart from it. No man has read aright the Father's word to the world in the Cross of Christ His Son, until he knows and feels that its message is that Love is supreme. This Song of Love therefore, is both deathless literature and immortal truth, and it may be summed up in this: "Every one that loveth is begotten of God." "If we love . . . God abideth in us." "He who abideth in love, abideth in God, and God abideth in him." Therefore, let us love.

But there is a final word in which,

4. A Course is Enjoined (14:1a)

"Follow after love." If it be asked *why* we should so do, the whole of chapter xiii is the answer. We should pursue love because the utmost ability and devotion apart from love are worthless (vv. 1-3); because the possession of love, even though unaccompanied by gifts, is the supreme good (vv. 4-7); because though all the gifts must pass away, love abides (vv. 8-12); and because even of those things which for ever remain, love is the greatest (v. 13).

And if it be asked *how* we may pursue love, the only answer is, by practising it.

If you ask: How can we practise such love as this? we are reminded that "the love of God is shed abroad in our hearts by the Holy Ghost." That brings us again to the very centre of all things, the manifestation of God in Christ, and the begetting of the likeness of Christ in the human soul by the Holy Spirit. His supreme work is to shed abroad this love in our hearts, wherewith we may love God our Creator, Redeemer, Saviour, and Sovereign, and also love one another.

Let me conclude with a simple story. My friend, Samuel Chadwick, now in the Lord's presence, has told this incident. One day in Leeds station he went into a waiting-room, and there was a man in the room; he was leaning against the mantelpiece and seemed in distress. Samuel Chadwick went up to him, and observed that he was weeping. He said: "My friend, are you in trouble?" "Not exactly," was the reply. "What is the matter, then?" asked Samuel Chadwick. "Well," he said, "my brother and I had saved a bit of money, and we thought we would start business, so we went to Crossley's and bought a gas engine, and put it into our little workshop to run it. After working for about two years, we found that we were losing money; the engine was not powerful enough for the task. So we decided to go back to the firm and explain the situation. We told the person we saw what had happened; that we were losing money; that the engine was not powerful enough, and asked what could be done "You got the engine you ordered, didn't you?" he said. "Yes." "I am afraid then we cannot do anything more." They left the office, and on the way out they met Frank Crossley. They addressed him, and told him the story. He took them back into his office, got all the particulars from them, and said: "Now, I will put an engine into your workshop adequate for the purpose, and if you will let me know what you have lost on that inadequate engine for the last two years, I will refund it to you." And the man wept again, and said: "Sir, I have seen the likest person to-day to Jesus Christ, and it has been too much for me."

The love life is the Christ life. The truth of this is forcefully brought out by reading *Christ*, as the Rev. Evan Hopkins once suggested, instead of *love*, throughout this chapter.

"Though I speak with the tongues of men and of angels, and have not Christ, I am become as sounding brass, or a tinkling cymbal. And though I have the gift of prophecy, and understand all mysteries, and all knowledge; and though I have all faith, so that I could remove mountains, and have not Christ, I am nothing. And though I bestow all my goods to feed the poor, and though I give my body to be burned, and have not Christ, it profiteth me nothing. Christ suffereth long, and is kind; Christ envieth not; Christ vaunteth not Himself, is not puffed up, doth not behave Himself unseemly, seeketh not His own, is not easily provoked, thinketh no evil; rejoiceth not in iniquity, but rejoiceth in the truth; beareth all things, believeth all things, hopeth all things, endureth all things. Christ never faileth."

He is the "same yesterday, to-day, and for ever," and as at last, when we shall see Him, we shall be like Him, it will be well for ourselves and for others if we become more like Him now.

Let each of us test himself by this sublime standard. No one of us, perhaps, will be able to go right through this programme, but each of us can go a little further in it every day.

I {
SUFFER LONG,
AM KIND,
ENVY NOT,
VAUNT NOT MYSELF,
AM NOT PUFFED UP,
DO NOT BEHAVE MYSELF UNSEEMLY,
SEEK NOT MY OWN,
AM NOT EASILY PROVOKED,
THINK NO EVIL,
REJOICE NOT IN INIQUITY,
REJOICE WITH THE TRUTH,
BEAR ALL THINGS
BELIEVE ALL THINGS,
HOPE ALL THINGS,
ENDURE ALL THINGS.

"Love Divine, all loves excelling,
　　Joy of heaven, to earth come down,
Fix in us Thy humble dwelling,
　　All Thy faithful mercies crown.

"Jesus, Thou art all compassion,
　　Pure unbounded love Thou art;
Visit us with Thy salvation,
　　Enter every trembling heart.

"Finish then Thy new creation;
　　Pure and spotless let it be;
Let us see Thy great salvation,
　　Perfectly restored in Thee.

"Changed from glory into glory,
　　Till in heaven we take our place,
Till we cast our crowns before Thee,
　　Lost in wonder, love, and praise!"